CREATING
a Glory
Atmosphere

CREATING a Glory Atmosphere

J. Darrel Turner

Empowered Publications Inc.
Millry, Alabama
www.empoweredpublicationsinc.com

Empowered Publications Inc.
529 County Road 31
Millry, Alabama 36558

Cover design by Christian Author Partner
Interior design by Christian Author Partner

Most Scripture quotations are taken from the King James Version of the Bible. However, there are a few quotations taken from the Amplified® Bible.

"Scripture quotations taken from the Amplified® Bible, Copyright © 1954, 1958, 1962, 1964, 1965, 1987 by The Lockman Foundation used by permission." (www.Lockman.org)

ISBN: 978-1-943033-06-5
Library of Congress Control Number: 2015946709

This book is dedicated to
my wife Gwen, and daughters
Chasmin and Danielle
who sacrificed the most
for me to go and do
the work of a Missionary Evangelist.

In memory of my Mother Ina Lee,
who when I was a Prodigal
"would not let me go".

TABLE OF CONTENTS

GLORY ATMOSPHERE

Chapter I

OVER the two thousand year span of Christendom there have been seasons of theological emphasis and experience. During the era of Martin Luther, the message of salvation by faith thru grace became the theme of born again scholars, and the experience of countless individuals around the globe as the wonderful revelation of divine truth was declared to the ignorant masses that had been kept in darkness by the Roman Church and its priests. During the times of John Wesley, the message of holiness and sanctification were boldly declared and the result was revival, a revival that not only impacted Europe, but America and beyond. During the early 1900s, the message was the Baptism of the Holy Ghost for all born again believers, and again the results were history changing as millions worldwide experienced the same infilling and anointing of the Holy Ghost as the early church had received on the day of Pentecost as recorded in Acts 2:1-4. It is believed by many that this *phenomena* of the Spirit ushered in what the scriptures calls the *last days* and the near-at-hand coming of Christ.

During the decades of the 30's, 40's and 50's there was a great emphasis placed on the biblical teaching of divine healing, miracles, and gifts of the Spirit, which again resulted in worldwide attention to the Pentecostal movement. Countless thousands were healed in tent crusades and other mass meetings in the United States and abroad. As with any revival or *move of God*, there were numbers of charlatans and phonies who preyed upon the hungry masses which brought a great reproach upon the Pentecostal and Spirit-filled movement. One could fill a book about the religious hucksters and frauds that fleeced the crowds for filthy lucre's sake. Demonstrating counterfeit miracles and often times preaching a compromised gospel.

During the late 70's and early 80's along with the increasing growth of the charismatic movement came a great emphasis on *praise and worship.* Across North America and around the world there were conferences and workshops on how to have a church where praise and worship were in some cases the *centerpiece* or focal point of the church service experience! To many, this was the *new thing* God was doing in the church, and it caught on like fire in a barn filled with hay! The common vernacular in the Pentecostal-Charismatic circles were things like *worship songs, worship team, worship leaders,* etc. There were countless books written and thousands of sermons preached on the subject of worship. The *praise and worship* phenomenon has become a theological subject and experience that will remain a vital part of latter day Christendom.

On the surface, a renewed emphasis on *praise and worship* in the church seemed a breath of fresh air after the stagnant atmosphere that permeated our Pentecostal churches when revival fires began to wane from the 1960's onward. For the most part, gone were the days when spontaneous worship would flow like a river out of hearts filled with life and the joy of the salvation of the lord in our services. Before modern Spirit-filled believers hung their harps on the willows, churches were filled with joyful praise and adoration to the

Lamb of Calvary. Long before even the ideal of a *worship team* or *worship leader,* Pentecostals were clapping and raising their hands with jubilant shouts of hallelujah, and praise you Jesus! Sadly, the decline of true joy, passion, holiness, and revival fervor, resulted in a Pentecostal church with little desire to worship the Creator of heaven and Earth. A great void was obvious and when the neo-Pentecostals began to emphasize praise and worship the *classical Pentecostals* reacted with resentment and countered with calling their praise and worship *fleshly and shallow.* While I am certain to expose myself to great criticism here, I must be honest in what I see and believe. There were—and no doubt are—many neo-Pentecostal Christians who truly worshipped God with a sincere and faithful heart, but I can also say that so many of their leaders have deemphasized the message of Bible holiness and godly living with their error-filled teaching and preaching. Many of the new and even some *classical Pentecostals* have preached a gospel message that makes a carnal life acceptable, and seemingly tolerated by God. So while the emphasis on *praise and worship* is needed in today's church, we must never forget the words of Jesus to the Samaritan woman at the well:

But the hour cometh, and now is, when the true worshippers shall worship the Father in spirit and in truth: for the Father seeketh such to worship Him. ~ John 4:23

Along with the emphasis on worshiping a Holy God should come the renewed emphasis on living and abiding in the grace and righteousness of Christ, and a commitment to living by the word of God. The soft attitude toward sin from the pulpit to the pew actually has cast a shadow on much of today's so-called worship. Hearts that are carnal and cold cannot produce a Glory Atmosphere with their praise. David said, those who ascend up to the "hill of the Lord" and "stand in His holy place" *WILL BE THOSE WHO...* "hath clean hands, and a pure heart; who hath not lifted up his soul unto vanity, nor sworn deceitfully." ~ Psalm 24:3-4

The common perception that God is pleased with worship and praise no matter from whom and where it comes from is promoted by religious stars both ministerial and from Hollywood. From the gaudy revivalist and progressive church pastor to the I-found-Jesus movie stars, so many act as if the Lord should be awed that they raise their hands and sing worship songs glorifying His name. To them, the Lord's umbrella is so large that it allows a broad array of beliefs and lifestyles to be accepted in the Father's house where worship is offered to a Holy God, but…

they that worship him must worship him in spirit and in truth. ~ John 4:24

Worship was to be from the very heart and soul of man. A heart that lives and desires to walk in obedience to God's divine truth, and in the grace of the Lord Jesus.

Just because there is a lot of praise in a service doesn't always mean that God is honored. Several years ago while sitting in a revival service, the Spirit of the Lord spoke to my heart saying, "Praise is not worship, unless it is accepted by God!" The children of Israel were worshipping whom they believed to be Jehovah as they danced around the golden calf. The problem was, their hard hearts were not in right relationship with God. Their praise was tainted with carnality and a religious vulgarity. Aaron said, they would worship and on the next day would have a *"feast unto the Lord."*

> **and the people sat down to eat and to drink, and rose up to play. ~ Exodus 32:6**

In many of today's churches and ministry circles the atmosphere is likened unto those services with the golden calf. Impurity, greed, creature worship, and a departure from truth are the Corinthian disasters of our time. Many are dancing, raising their hands, swaying with the music, and saying how much they love Jesus, but as the Lord said:

> **This people draweth nigh unto me with their mouth, and honoureth me with their lips; but their heart is far from me. ~ Matthew 15:8**

The great tragedy of our time is that while men proclaim, "God is in the house," the atmosphere is such that His presence cannot dwell among us. The great need of this hour in the modern church are a people who offer praise and worship that creates a "Glory Atmosphere."

DOES ATMOSPHERE MATTER?

Chapter II

WEBSTER defines atmosphere as "a surrounding influence or environment." Obviously, in the spiritual or natural sense this influence or environment can be good or bad, positive or negative, and in the spirit realm, godly or demonic.

Does atmosphere really matter when it comes to spiritual matters? I am convinced it does, and actually scripturally convinced; thus the purpose of this book. I was brought up in what we would term an *old fashioned* classical Pentecostal church. Most of the members were coal miners or their direct descendants. Irish roots ran deep, and the people worked hard and long hours to provide the necessities of life for their families. For the Christians in the community, going to the house of God was as much a part of their lives as eating and breathing. The services were long and lively! I can remember as a boy the Sunday night service concluding about the same time as the second-shift workers were getting home from their jobs.

While much of my young life was not centered on spiritual matters, I learned some very important present and eternal truths in those services among the Pentecostals. One of the greatest was that atmosphere and environment does matter. I've often stated while preaching that one of the great reasons I believe so few believers receive the baptism in the Holy Ghost in present times is the absence of a Holy Ghost atmosphere! While what I am about to say might seem overly simplistic, elementary, and even somewhat trivial to some, I am convinced that there is a great spiritual truth and reality in it.

In the 1960s and 70s, and I'm sure prior to my birth and life, when hungry believers would go to the altars to pray and seek to be filled with the baptism in the Holy Ghost, they were *always* surrounded by Spirit-filled Christians who were there to *pray them through*! It was not a *watch-the-clock*, I've got to get up early for work tomorrow type prayer; most were there for the duration.

They prayed with the seeker until they were filled or simply *worn out*, and got up determined to keep praying for the promised Spirit in the next service, or even at home. Even in the early 1980s, before I was traveling very much in the ministry, my wife and I would stay around the altars in our church praying for hungry seekers till after midnight at times. Rarely was there anyone who sincerely wanted to be filled who went very long without being gloriously baptized in the precious Holy Spirit of God!

Let me describe the atmosphere in that country church setting. Hungry hearts kneeling at the altar praying earnestly for the baptism in the Holy Ghost, the singers were singing glorious songs under the anointing, and the musicians were playing as if for the Lord Himself. Much of the congregation would be gathered around the seekers, with both praying fervently! Those praying for the earnest seekers would usually lay their hands on them saying something like, "Oh God, fill our brother, our sister with the Holy Ghost in the mighty name of Jesus!" Yes some were demonstrative in their praying and laying on of hands. Was this necessary for the seeker to be filled? No, but there is nothing wrong with sincere fervent prayer from true believers.

> **Confess your faults one to another, and pray one for another, that ye may be healed. The effectual fervent prayer of a righteous man availeth much.**
> **~ James 5:16**

The amplified states the verse: "*The earnest (heartfelt, continued) prayer of a righteous man makes tremendous power available [dynamic in its working]*. Barnes in his commentary says about fervent prayer; "it is not listless, indifferent, cold, lifeless, as if there were no vitality in it, or power, but that which is adapted to be efficient - earnest, sincere, hearty."

I do not at all want to imply that loud, emotional, demonstrative praying is what brings the blessing, but I do believe such fervent praying helped create an atmosphere where hungry seekers could be filled with the Holy Ghost. The modern preacher might dismiss such, but with so few truly being baptized in the Spirit in our day of dry services, quiet altars, and rarely anyone praying the fervent prayer of a righteous man, what happened? The spiritual atmosphere in most Pentecostal churches does not help create an environment conducive for hungry seekers to be filled with the Spirit, resulting in one of the great tragedies of the modern church. In the two major Pentecostal denominations in America, less than *twenty percent* of the members claim the baptism in the Holy Ghost. I cast no stones. This is the case in every Pentecostal movement, and most (with some exceptions) non-denominational churches that consider themselves Pentecostal in doctrine and experience. The great Pentecostal movement of the latter day was born in Holy Ghost revival where the atmosphere was conducive for believers to be filled.

In the Old Testament, there is a great case in point of how the spiritual atmosphere can be affected by anointed worship and music. It is found in the story of King Saul and the anointed shepherd by the name of David. After King Saul had disobeyed God's commandments and grieved the Holy Spirit, the Holy Spirit departed from the King. Then an evil Spirit came and would at times torment Saul. He could find no relief. Finally, one of the King's men said;

Let our lord now command thy servants, which are before thee, to seek out a man, who is a cunning player on an harp: and it shall come to pass, when the evil spirit from God is upon thee, that he shall play with his hand, and thou shalt be well.
~ I Samuel 16:16

And it came to pass, when the evil spirit from God was upon Saul, that David took an harp, and played with his hand: so Saul was refreshed, and was well, and the evil spirit departed from him.
~ I Samuel 16:23

It wasn't just talent and skill that drove the evil spirit from Saul. It was the anointed hand of David that the Spirit of God rested upon. When he played under the anointing the atmosphere became such that the evil spirit fled. The devil and his spirits of darkness cannot dwell long in a Holy Ghost atmosphere!

Another case in point was found when King Jehoshaphat and the vile King Joram came to Elisha for a prophetic word from God. Elisha was vexed at the very sight of King Joram and was in no mood to have church! Elisha then said, "but now bring me a minstrel. And it came to pass, when the minstrel played, that the hand of the LORD came upon him." (2 Kings. 3:15)

Adam Clark in his great old commentary said, "'Bring me a minstrel' – A person who played on the harp. The rabbis, and many Christians, suppose that Elisha's mind was considerably irritated and grieved by the bad behavior of the young men at Bethel, and their tragic end, and by the presence of the idolatrous king of Israel; and therefore called for Divine psalmody, that it might calm his spirits, and render him more susceptible of the prophetic influence. To be able to discern the voice of God, and the operation of his hand, it is necessary that the mind be calm, and the passions all in harmony, under the direction of reason; that reason may be under the influence of the Divine Spirit."

YES, ATMOSPHERE DOES MATTER!

CREATING A GLORY ATMOSPHERE
Chapter III

I know many fatalist Christians will ask, "How can we create an atmosphere of glory?" Since God is Sovereign, He goes and comes when He pleases. What could we as finite beings ever do that would provide an environment where the presence of the Infinite God of the universe would want to dwell among us?

Yet these same Christians will announce a special time of daily prayer for the upcoming revival scheduled for the church, or call for a time of prayer before the Sunday night service. There are some that will go as far as to promote a period of fasting before special meetings and events. My question to these who believe we cannot do anything to enhance or create the atmosphere where we need and desire God to work is: Why bother? Why pray? Why fast? Since God is Sovereign, why not just come together and have the meeting or event and just hope God shows up and blesses us, and what we are doing. If we don't believe that with our prayer, fasting, and faith we can move God to manifest Himself in a special way, then why waste our time? Are we just doing it because of tradition, because that's what we've always done?

When it comes to praying, fasting, and worship, have we really thought about the *why* in a deeper sense than just tradition, or just because the Bible tells us too?

From the night I was born again, I've been a worshiper of God. Having been reared in a Pentecostal church, I knew that worshipping and giving Him praise was what real Christians did and desired to do! I heard it preached how the Lord was worthy to be praised, and that it would bring blessings to the believer and the church that would consistently worship Him. Yet in all the years I attended church services as a boy, and the thirty-five years—at the time of this writing—since I was born again, I had never really heard anyone preach or teach, nor did I read any writings on the *why*. On the why that went beyond what I had heard and read most of my life, and when God showed me this great Biblical truth it revolutionized my understanding of worship.

This deeper understanding of Glory Atmosphere, how and why it's created is so clearly seen in Isaiah's experience of seeing the glory of God in the Temple. "In the year that king Uzziah died I saw also the Lord sitting upon a throne, high and lifted up, and his train filled the temple. Above it stood the seraphims: each one had six wings; with twain he covered his face, and with twain he covered his feet, and with twain he did fly. And one cried unto another, and said, Holy, holy, holy, is the LORD of hosts: the whole earth is full of his glory. And the posts of the door moved at the voice of him that cried, and the house was filled with smoke." (Isaiah 6:1-4)

In this holy atmosphere, the prophet of God saw the Lord, high and lifted up with his train, or the skirts of His garment, filling the temple. Who did he see? The Lord! Most of the old commentators say that the One he saw was the Christ. Matthew Henry wrote in his great commentary "that Isaiah saw not Jehovah—the essence of God (no man has seen that, or can see it), but Adonai—his dominion. He saw the Lord Jesus; so this vision is explained in John 12:41. That Isaiah now saw Christ's glory and spoke of him, which is an incontestable proof of the divinity of our Saviour. He it is who when, after his resurrection, he sat down on the right hand of God, did but sit down where he was before."

And now, O Father, glorify thou me with thine own self with the glory which I had with thee before the world was.
~ John 17:5

When we Christians read or hear the word *glory* we think almost exclusively of smoke, fire, lights, etc. These are often the manifestations of *glory*, but not necessarily glory. These can be found many places throughout scripture where God's presence is manifested, like the burning bush in the desert that caught Moses's attention. As the children of Israel was traversing the wilderness, they saw a *pillar* of fire by night, and a *cloud* of glory by day, and *smoke* and *fire* in Exodus 19:18.

While there may be places in scripture where we find the presence of God without these particular manifestations, I am convinced that He will not be found anywhere there is no **Glory Atmosphere!** Some years ago, when I was preparing a sermon on worship, the Lord began to show me the most wonderful truths about what happens when we truly praise and worship Him. My journey started in Isaiah's experience here in chapter six:

> **In the year that king Uzziah died I saw also the Lord sitting upon a throne, high and lifted up, and his train filled the temple. Above it stood the seraphims: each one had six wings; with twain he covered his face, and with twain he covered his feet, and with twain he did fly. And one cried unto another, and said, Holy, holy, holy, is the LORD of hosts: the whole earth is full of his glory. And the posts of the door moved at the voice of him that cried, and the house was filled with smoke.**
> **~ Isaiah 6:1-4**

These Seraphim or angelic creatures are called, "Seraphim burners." Some state that they have a brazen fiery appearance. They burn in love and zeal to create an atmosphere for God to dwell and abide in. They were created for this glory. This is how they minister to Him!

Who maketh...; his ministers a flaming fire: ~ Psalms 104:4

In these verses they are facing each other with two of their six wings covering their faces. Adonai, the Lord, is sitting on a throne in between them as they continually cry aloud, "Holy, holy, holy, is the LORD of hosts: the whole earth is full of His glory." Then the other one cries back "Holy, holy, holy, is the LORD of hosts: the whole earth is full of His glory." This worship is unceasing. The atmosphere between them where the Lord is seated on His throne is saturated with praise and Glory. What are they doing? They are giving Him glory, and as they do the atmosphere becomes a *Glory Atmosphere*. Some might say that it is not illogical for angelic beings to *give God glory*, as they are supernatural beings created for such a wonderful thing. But we are mere mortals and we could never give God anything that would create an atmosphere for Him to dwell in. That is exactly what we are commanded to do in Holy Scriptures. In fact, I will give several verses that will certainly show us God's will concerning our part in all this.

> **Glory and honour are in his presence; strength and gladness are in his place. Give unto the LORD, ye kindreds of the people, give unto the LORD glory and strength. Give unto the LORD the glory due unto his name: bring an offering, and come before him: worship the LORD in the beauty of holiness.**
> **~ I Chronicles 16:27-29**

Glory and honour are in His presence according to verse 27, so without doubt the two go together. How does this glory get there? Verses 28 and 29 the people of God are commanded to give Him this glory; glory that is due unto his name. Giving glory, offering, and worship are all tied together. Worship is a way we give Him glory, and one way we worship is by giving an offering!

Give unto the LORD the glory due unto his name: bring an offering and come into his courts. ~ Psalms 96:8

Some years back, at our ministries' annual **Fire on the Mountain** camp meeting in Tennessee, we had a phenomenal experience in relation to worship, giving, and bringing an offering to the Lord. Facing a huge budget for the expenses of the meeting, I was praying earnestly for God to give us a miracle in the offerings. By the middle of the camp meeting, we were still far from meeting our expenses. During one of the services, as the man of God was preaching on the woman who came into a house where Jesus was visiting carrying an alabaster box of ointment, something began to stir in the hearts of those in the service. The minister dealt with the story of this woman as an individual who was giving this ointment as praise, worship, and an offering unto Jesus. Those in attendance began to worship and praise the Lord as the message stirred their hearts, and then the Spirit of God began to move in an unusual way. Someone rose up from their seat and went to the back of the building where the offering buckets had been stored. They brought one and set it on the stage while the man of God was still preaching. The sounds of praise and worship rose higher, and without anyone saying anything about giving a monetary offering, people began to walk up to the stage and drop their offering into the bucket that had been placed there. What a sight! The man of God kept right on preaching. The people were worshiping and praising God with their voices, and at the same time the offering bucket is being filled with gifts from hearts that are giving Him glory with praise and offerings. In that service, several thousand dollars were given for the budget of the meeting, but that wasn't the only miracle. There were divine healings that took place as well as the Lord moving and meeting many needs among His people! I believed before this incident, but certainly afterwards. I've never doubted that giving an offering is as much a form of worship as raising our hands and shouting hallelujah!

Whether in heaven or in earth, this glory is to be given by God's creation. In the heavens, His angelic host give Him glory.

And when those beasts give glory and honour and thanks

to him that sat on the throne, who liveth for ever and ever, ~ Revelation 4:9

An angel will fly over the earth in Revelation 14:7 and declare, "Saying with a loud voice, Fear God, and give glory to him; for the hour of his judgment is come: and worship him that made heaven, and earth, and the sea, and the fountains of waters."

This giving Him glory is creating an atmosphere for God to dwell in. This will become clearer as we continue deeper into God's word. God only dwells in *Glory Atmosphere*, and His creation—whether celestial or terrestrial—have a part in creating it.

HOW DO WE BRING HIM GLORY?

Chapter IV

HOW does bringing glory create an atmosphere where God will show up, abide, and dwell in? Let us look again at Isaiah's experience in the temple.

In the year that king Uzziah died I saw also the Lord sitting upon a throne, high and lifted up, and his train filled the temple. ~ Isaiah 6:1

Who did he see? The Lord, *Adonai*—Christ in the Old Testament.

The great old commentary Jamieson-Fausset-Brown states, "Isaiah could only have 'seen' the Son, not the divine essence. 'No man hath seen

God at any time; the only begotten Son, which is in the bosom of the Father, he hath declared him, John 1:18.' John declared Him to be the Christ that Isaiah saw in John 12:41. These things said Esaias, when he saw his glory, and spake of him."

What happened in Isaiah chapter six also is taking place in the heavens with the Cherubim in Revelation 4:8, "And the four beasts had each of them six wings about him; and they were full of eyes within: and they rest not day and night, saying, Holy, holy, holy, Lord God Almighty, which was, and is, and is to come."

What were they doing? They were giving Him *glory* and *honor*! They were creating an atmosphere for the God of the universe to dwell in, yet they aren't the only creatures in scripture giving Him glory and creating *Glory Atmosphere.*

The four and twenty elders fall down before him that sat on the throne, and worship him that liveth for ever and ever, and cast their crowns before the throne, saying, Thou art worthy, O Lord, to

receive glory and honour and power: for thou hast created all things, and for thy pleasure they are and were created. ~ Revelation 4:10-11

I must admit that when I read verse 11, I was puzzled and actually pushed my chair back from my desk. I said to the Lord, "I understand and see how that angelic beings, heavenly saints and true worshippers can give you glory and honor, but how can any being in heaven or in earth give power to the one who already has all power in heaven and in earth?" I said to the Lord, "I need some scriptural understanding of this, and I really cannot proceed until You help me to grasp this *giving you power* part of the verse."

At that moment my mind was taken back to when Moses and the children of Israel were in a great battle against Amalek in the seventeenth chapter of Exodus. When the battle started Moses was standing on the top of a hill with the rod of God in his hand outstretched. As long as Moses held out the rod of God, the battle went in favor of the children of Israel, but when his arms became weak and lowered, the battle favored

Amalek. Then Aaron and Hur put a stone under his arms to keep them up till the going down of the sun. What was the significance of the rod being held up toward heaven—Godward?

That rod wasn't just any old stick! According to the ancient customs of the Nomadic tribes, when a young man started his journey in life, he received a staff that had been made of wood, preserved by the oil of animals. Starting on the bottom of that staff he would carve some kind of mark signifying significant times in his life. It was not just a walking cane, but also a testimony of the blessings and miraculous events wrought by God. These markings on the staff reminded him of the great and wonderful things the Lord had done. So when Moses held up that rod, he was holding up a testimony to the great and mighty things God had done in bringing the children of Israel out of Egypt and through the wilderness. As he held this rod high as a symbol of worship and thanksgiving to God, he was giving God glory, and in giving Him glory, he was creating an atmosphere for the mighty power of God to work on behalf of Israel. He wasn't giving God power, but an atmosphere for God's power to work!

Then I prayed, "Lord, give me something else." And my mind was taken to a time where Jesus was visiting among his own kinsman and childhood neighbors.

And He did not many mighty works there because of their unbelief. ~ Matthew 15:38

Here Jesus did few signs and wonders among His own people because their unbelief created an atmosphere that hindered the power of God from working. They could not give Him power nor take away His power, but they could create an atmosphere for it to work, or not work!

WHAT HAPPENS IN GLORY ATMOSPHERE?

Chapter V

I AM convinced that God only lives in, dwells, and inhabits a *Glory Atmosphere*! All my life in the church, I heard a verse of scripture quoted with different wording than what was actually written in the Bible. The verse was always quoted: "The Bible says, 'God inhabits the praises of His people.'" Actually, that's not the way it is written in the Bible. The actual Bible verse is:

> **But thou art holy, O thou that inhabitest the praises of Israel.**
> **~ Psalms 22:3**

Now let me state clearly that while it's not written in the particular wording, ninety-nine percent of believers and ministers quote it. There's no doubt it means the same for us the church, as for ancient Israel. My argument for that is clear. God dwells in *Glory Atmosphere*, and praise and true worship create those conditions.

The word *Inhabitest* comes from the Hebrew word *yaw-shab'*—a primitive root; properly to sit down (specifically as judge, in ambush, in quiet); by implication to dwell, to remain.

When the Israelites were in right standing with God, and would praise and worship Jehovah, an atmosphere was created where He would come and dwell, abide, sit down like a judge, in ambush, as if waiting to do something. Isaiah said, "I saw also the Lord sitting upon a throne." The word "sitting" is the same Hebrew word "*yaw-shab*" as inhabitest in Psalm 22:3.

What is He doing sitting on His throne? What does any king do while sitting on the royal throne of their kingdom? They are bringing righteous judgment and working on behalf of their people. Good and righteous kings obviously were concerned about the needs of their subjects, and were occupied with making decrees for their welfare. From all appearances of any thrones of ancient past, they were not comfortable, they were not for rest or leisure.

So being assured that God does dwell and inhabit the praises of His people, what does that fully mean for us as true worshippers? This may seem quite elementary to some, but for me quite intriguing and encouraging. Some years ago, I was meditating on Psalm 22:3, and the Hebrew renderings of the word *inhabitest*. These were my thoughts. Somewhere in a church service (could be anywhere people are gathered), the people of God begin to praise and magnify God in true worship from hearts in love with Jesus. I could see the worship going up to the presence of the Lord. As Adonai begins to smell this sweet savor of praise and worship coming from His people, I could hear Him say, "Bring My chariot. I have somewhere to go." Now some will say, "Wait a minute! What makes you think God has a chariot?" Actually, He has several.

For, behold, the LORD will come with fire, and with his chariots like a whirlwind,
~ Isaiah 66:15

who maketh the clouds His chariot: ~ Psalm 104:3

I could hear the heavenly host saying, "Where are you going, oh Lord?" In my mind I heard His reply, "To earth, to the church, to dwell among the people who are praising Me, who are giving Me Glory and honour and power." I could see the Lord riding that chariot down and pulling up to the sanctuary where that body of believers was giving Him glory, and where a *Glory Atmosphere* was being created by their praise and true worship.

Oh, how many times I've said when preaching and telling this to the audience, "You may not see Him when He gets here, but you'll know when He shows up! What has He come to do? To save our lost, heal the sick and afflicted, set captives free, bring sight to the blind, heal the broken hearted, and baptize hungry hearts with the baptism in the Holy Ghost!"

Elementary? To some I'm sure, but to me it's phenomenal!

Oh, how we need Adonai to show up in these modern times, and the only way is for the people of God to start giving Him Glory due to His worthy name! Our *pittance* praise, and *cut and paste* worship has hindered the presence of the Lord from coming to dwell in our meetings, our homes, or wherever we need God to show up!

EXAMPLES OF GOD SHOWING UP

(THE DAY OF PENTECOST)

Chapter VI

MANY scholars believe that the day of Pentecost was when the New Testament church was born. Others say it was on the day of Christ's death on the cross, and still some teach the church was born on the day of our Lord's resurrection.

I am in the day of Pentecost camp—when the Holy Spirit came and empowered a group of faltering, powerless believers, and turned them into living and burning witnesses for Christ and His resurrection.

The disciples had been commanded.

And, behold, I send the promise of my Father upon you: but tarry ye in the city of Jerusalem, until ye be endued with power from on high. ~ Luke 24:49

Little did they realize that this *tarrying* would be more than just sitting and waiting on the promise. They would from seven to ten days be creating an atmosphere for the promised Spirit to descend into. Actually, they would start before they even reached Jerusalem. For after they beheld Him as He ascended heavenward the Bible declares:

And they worshipped Him, and returned to Jerusalem with great joy: And were continually in the temple, praising and blessing God. Amen ~ Luke 24:52-53

It is without doubt that they were giving Him glory, praise, and honor from the moment they watched Him ascend, while on their journey back to Jerusalem, and the days preceding Pentecost. This giving Him glory and worship from hearts filled with *great joy* over a period of days (there is debate among scholars on whether it was seven or ten days) caused the atmosphere to change. Now some would say, "What was wrong with the atmosphere?" When we look back to times leading up to Jesus's arrest, death and resurrection, we find some things that happened that no doubt left lingering *feelings* among these disciples, who had been struggling with their flesh and each other.

We remember that the sons of thunder— James and John—came with their mother to Jesus desiring to be seated on His left and right side in the future Kingdom. This created no small stir or feelings among the others, for the scripture states:

> **And when they heard it, they were moved with indignation against the two brethren.**
> **~ Matthew 20:24**

Strong's Greek rendering of *indignation* means: to be "greatly afflicted" and "sorely displeased!" This wound was not easily, nor soon healed!

It is no doubt the *brave* words of Peter were still fresh in the minds of his brethren from the night of Jesus's betrayal. Peter—*the rock*—adamantly said to the Lord,

> **Though I should die with thee, yet will I not deny thee.**
> **~ Matthew 26:35**

Of course, before the cock crew, he had cursed and denied Him three times! I am certain that each time they looked at Peter, his cowardly words echoed in their minds.

Then we have the stinging words of Thomas to the other disciples after they had proclaimed to him that they had seen the Lord. He met their *joy filled* proclamation with unbelief.

> **Except I shall see in His hands the print of the nails, and put my finger into the print of the nails, and thrust my hand into His side, I will not believe.**
> **~ John 20:25**

This harsh rebuke of their testimony surely

lingered in their wounded hearts. I am also convinced that some of them, if not all, struggled with jealousy over the fact that the first one to see Jesus after His resurrection and to proclaim the gospel of a risen Savior was a woman. Not just any woman, but one whom Jesus had cast out seven devils—Mary Magdalene. In a time when Middle Eastern culture relegated the status of women below men, and before the writings of Paul the Apostle.

there is neither male nor female: for ye are all one in Christ Jesus. ~ Galatians 3:28

Jesus did the unthinkable and conversed with a woman with a *past* before He appeared to His hand-picked male disciples!

These followers of Jesus along with their *issues* were sent to Jerusalem to tarry for the promised Spirit. Thankfully, they prayed and no doubt fasted during those seven to ten days; but that's not all. They worshiped Him and continually were praising and blessing God. So whatever issues they had in their hearts were dealt with in prayer, and their worship began to change the atmosphere into a *Glory Atmosphere* where the presence of God could dwell. It became such an atmosphere where the Holy Ghost could descend into, and He did! After these days of prayer, praise, worship, and creating Glory Atmosphere something happened!

And when the day of Pentecost was fully come, they were all with one accord in one place. And suddenly there came a sound from heaven as of a rushing mighty wind, and it filled all the house where they were sitting. And there appeared unto them cloven tongues like as of fire, and it sat upon each of them. And they were all filled with the Holy Ghost, and began to speak with other tongues, as the Spirit gave them utterance. ~ Acts 2:1-4

In this *Glory Atmosphere* God came to dwell, abide, sit, and fill the vessels of one hundred twenty hungry, glory-giving followers of Christ! There was a sound from heaven. It shook the whole city, which was overflowing with the faithful from around the world who had come to Jerusalem to celebrate the time of harvest.

These pilgrims and dwellers of Jerusalem were in the streets celebrating in type and shadow, but the disciples were in the upper room experiencing reality. Things happen when God comes to dwell in Glory Atmosphere. On this day, the beginning of the fulfillment of Joel's prophecy was fulfilled:

> **And it shall come to pass in the last days, saith God, I will pour out of My Spirit upon all flesh: and your sons and your daughters shall prophesy, and your young men shall see visions, and your old men shall dream dreams: And on My servants and on My handmaidens I will pour out in those days of My Spirit; and they shall prophesy.**
> **~ Acts 2:17-18**

A formerly backslidden disciple, who had promised faithfulness, who then ran, denied, and cursed, stands up, and boldly begins to proclaim the Gospel. He brings the crowd under the sentence of judgment for having the blood of the *Just One* on their hands, and then responds with mercy to their plea, "What shall we do?" Before the day is over, one hundred and twenty disciples and believers are baptized in the Holy Ghost. Peter shakes a city with the first Spirit empowered message of the New Testament church, and three thousand Jews from around the known world cry out for God's mercy and forgiveness which results in their salvation! Hallelujah! God comes to dwell in *Glory Atmosphere* and miraculous things happen when He does!

PRAYER AND PRAISE
Chapter VII

THIS praise, worship, and giving God glory continue in the early days of the church. Even their prayers were filled with praise and worship, and therefore created an atmosphere where God would come. After the miracle of the lame man in Acts chapter three, and their arrest for teaching the people the resurrection through Jesus Christ, they were threatened and released.

The word of God gives us a glorious look into what happens when prayer and praise create Glory Atmosphere.

And being let go, they went to their own company, and reported all that the chief priests and elders had said unto

them. And when they heard that, they lifted up their voice to God with one accord, and said, Lord, thou art God, which hast made heaven, and earth, and the sea, and all that in them is: Who by the mouth of thy servant David hast said, Why did the heathen rage, and the people imagine vain things? The kings of the earth stood up, and the rulers were gathered together against the Lord, and against His Christ. For of a truth against Thy holy child Jesus, whom Thou hast anointed, both Herod, and Pontius Pilate, with the Gentiles, and the people of Israel, were gathered together, For to do whatsoever Thy hand and Thy counsel determined before to be done. And now, Lord, behold their threatenings: and grant unto Thy servants, that with all boldness they may speak Thy word, By stretching forth Thine

hand to heal; and that signs and wonders may be done by the name of Thy holy child Jesus. And when they had prayed, the place was shaken where they were assembled together; and they were all filled with the Holy Ghost, and they spake the word of God with boldness. ~ Acts 4:23-31

When God's people begin to give Him glory and praise as Creator of heaven and earth, something begins to change in the atmosphere!

It happened in the Old Testament as well. When God was glorified and given credit for making all things in creation, He no doubt was well pleased and came to dwell in those praises. We see this when Solomon was dedicating the temple, and in his prayer and praise He gives God glory as the creator, which creates *Glory Atmosphere* and God coming down!

For Solomon had made a brasen scaffold, of five cubits long, and five cubits broad, and

three cubits high, and had set it in the midst of the court: and upon it he stood, and kneeled down upon his knees before all the congregation of Israel, and spread forth his hands toward heaven. ~ II Chronicles 6:13

Here the great king of Israel bows down in the posture of worship to give God glory.

O LORD God of Israel, there is no God like thee in the heaven, nor in the earth; ~ II Chronicles 6:14

Often in prayer I've thought of the words of Solomon, "there is no God like Thee." I have said to the Lord, "Not only is there no God like Thee, but there is no God but You!"

After Solomon in the position of worship begins to give God glory in his prayer, something glorious happens. I believe the Chariot pulls up!

Now when Solomon had made an end of praying, the fire

came down from heaven, and consumed the burnt offering and the sacrifices; and the glory of the LORD filled the house. And the priests could not enter into the house of the LORD, because the glory of the LORD had filled the LORD's house. And when all the children of Israel saw how the fire came down, and the glory of the LORD upon the house, they bowed themselves with their faces to the ground upon the pavement, and worshipped, and praised the LORD, saying, For He is good; for His mercy endureth for ever.
~ II Chronicles 7:1-3

I believe in these last days the *Big Bang Intellectuals* have become militant in their denial of God's hand in creation. Not only are the halls of higher learning saturated with big bang theory teaching, but in most elementary schools children are taught that there was no God involved in creating the heavens and the earth. The message of fools dominate modern teaching and thinking.

The fool hath said in his heart, there is no God. ~ Psalm 53:1

I am convinced that when the people of God in spirit and truth begin to give Him praise and glory as the creator of the heavens and earth and all that in them is, it moves the heart of God to come and dwell among those He created and who are the "apple of His eye!"

CREATING GLORY AT MIDNIGHT
Chapter VIII

BY this time, I am sure most reading this book are rejoicing in these great truths concerning worship and Glory Atmosphere. Yet the mere mention of the word *midnight* can cast a shadow over the revelation of God's word to our heart. The word is often associated with darkness, despair, and hopelessness. We can get excited about the Seraphim and Cherubim giving glory and creating Glory Atmosphere. Our hearts rejoice at the reading of how Solomon prayed and worshiped, and then saw fire fall from heaven as God came to dwell in their midst at the dedication. The same with the day of Pentecost, and in early church prayer meetings. But again, there's something about *midnight* and its association with darkness, trials, and suffering that takes some of the joy out of it. If this glorious truth won't work in the *midnight* times of our lives, then it's a very fragile truth indeed!

Some would say that it's one thing to worship God in church services where people are praising and giving Him glory in corporate unison. It's acceptable that we can praise Him in a prayer meeting where the atmosphere is charged with believers praying and praising the Lord. Even when we are alone somewhere just raising our hands and worshipping in spirit and in truth, we can see that an atmosphere can be created where God comes and dwells in. Yet, there are those who would say that there are some *midnight* situations where this might not work. There are some places where the atmosphere is so bad, so sin-tainted that God might not show up, because we do know that He is holy!

Yes, God is holy and I am convinced He will only dwell in a holy atmosphere. That's why even in the *midnight* times, when the atmosphere is not *Glory Atmosphere*, we have to create it. Right now you're saying, "You better have a scriptural basis for stating that." I do, and it is found in the sixteenth chapter of Acts.

Paul and Silas are on their way to a prayer meeting. A young damsel who has for days consistently followed them declared, "These men are the servants of the most high God, which shew unto us the way of salvation." She was a fortuneteller who worked for certain men of the city, and seemingly made them a lot of money. After a few days of her following Paul and Silas, the Apostle Paul was grieved and turned, and commanded the spirit of divination to come out of her. When her masters saw that their means of profit were gone, they had Paul and Silas arrested. After this they were beaten, placed in stocks, and bonds, and put down in the inner prison or the dungeon.

While the Jews under Roman law were forbidden to administer over forty stripes, these men were under no such restrictions. No doubt their wounds were many and deep. The jailer put their feet in stocks, perhaps wooden instruments secured with chains. In the old commentary Jamieson, Fausset, and Brown we read, "pestilential cells, damp and cold, from which the light was excluded, and where the chains rusted on the prisoners." There is perhaps no way for our modern minds (especially in the United

States) to comprehend how bad the atmosphere was surrounding the great Apostle and his young helper in the Lord. They were in the inner prison, the dungeon, with no windows. The air was filled with the stench of numbers of wretched prisoners. There were some with infections that were rotting the flesh, as well as diseases that filled the air with a putrid smell of impending death. Human waste was left, no doubt, for days on end. Rats and insects filled the dungeon. You could hear the screams of the dying, and the cursing of those chained in this inner hell. That, dear friend, is certainly not *Glory Atmosphere*! It isn't the kind of place where you would expect God to show up and manifest His divine power. The only hope Paul and Silas had for deliverance was to change the atmosphere around them. That is exactly what they did.

And at midnight Paul and Silas prayed, and sang praises unto God. ~ Acts 16:23

There is something about *midnight* when the rays of sunlight have been absent for many hours, and when the morning seems so far away. I'm sure Paul had read what Job said, "...who giveth songs in the night;" (Job 35:10).

Someone would ask, "Do you believe that Paul was actually aware that God dwells in *Glory Atmosphere*, and was actually praying and singing praises unto the Lord in the prison to change things?" Yes, and yes. I believe if anyone knew these great truths, it would have been him. He knew what happened in Isaiah's experience in the temple. He has studied and read often the experience of Solomon when he was dedicating the temple, and no doubt had heard the testimonies of what happened on the Day of Pentecost numerous times. In fact, I am certain it was Paul himself that was referenced in the following scripture.

> **I knew a man in Christ above fourteen years ago, (whether in the body, I cannot tell; or whether out of the body, I cannot tell: God knoweth;) such an one caught up to the third heaven. And I knew such a man, (whether in the body, or out of the body, I cannot tell: God knoweth;) How that he**

was caught up into paradise, and heard unspeakable words, which it is not lawful for a man to utter. ~ II Corinthians 12:2-4

Therefore Paul had witnessed in the heavenly realm how the Cherubim cried out "Holy, holy, holy, Lord God Almighty, which was, and is, and is to come." (Revelation 4:8) He had heard the four and twenty elders creating Glory Atmosphere in Revelation 11:16. So he certainly understood what happens in *Glory Atmosphere.*

So at midnight, Paul and Silas begin to pray and sing praises. The Greek for *praises* here means hymn. Some of the old commentators believe they were singing Psalm 113 to 118 which was known by Jewish believers of the day. It could have been included in the hymn Jesus and the disciples sang on the night of Passover. Whatever the song, they *sang praises unto God.* Without doubt, they were singing and praising loudly, because it stated: "…the prisoners heard them."

They were giving God glory and honor and power, and while they were giving Him glory something began to change in the atmosphere around them. It became holy. It became *Glory Atmosphere.* And just like in the temple in Isaiah's day where the posts of the door moved, and in the prayer meeting in Acts 4:31 where the foundation of the house was shaken, things went to shaking around the dungeon.

> **And suddenly there was a great earthquake, so that the foundations of the prison were shaken: and immediately all the doors were opened, and every one's bands were loosed.**
> **~ Acts 16:26**

Hallelujah! Even in our darkest hour and trial, we can begin to give God glory and change our gloomy, dark, and desperate atmosphere to one of *Glory Atmosphere*. And He will show up!

Some would say, "Do you really believe the atmosphere changed? Absolutely! I personally believe the cursing of those prisoners stopped. In fact, I believe something spiritually happened to them when the presence of God came into that prison. If you think I am taking that too far, let me tell you why. It stated, "every one's bands were loosed." I am certain that the men in the dungeon were the worst of the worst, and likely on death row, or deemed high risk. Anyone knows that bad men would have run away and escaped. Even the jailer assumed such as he was about to fall on his own sword thinking he was going to be held accountable for a massive jailbreak. Yet, nobody ran! Everybody remained in the dungeon. Surely something wonderful and supernatural happened to these formerly accursed criminals!

Revival broke out in the jail and conviction arrested the heart of the jailer. He went from wanting to take his life to wanting eternal life. The jailer brought them out, and said, "Sirs, what must I do to be saved?" During a hastily called revival service Paul and Silas preached Christ to the jailer and "all that were in his house." Before the sun came up, they were all baptized in water!

How is it possible to go from such an anti-God, dark atmosphere to *Glory Atmosphere* where the power of God shakes the building, liberates the captives, supernaturally touches the criminals, and saves the jailer and his whole household all between midnight and sunrise?

Paul and Silas prayed and sang praises… ~ Acts 16:25

IN THE GREAT BATTLE OF LIFE

Chapter IX

It came to pass after this also, that the children of Moab, and the children of Ammon, and with them other beside the Ammonites, came against Jehoshaphat to battle. Then there came some that told Jehoshaphat, saying, There cometh a great multitude against thee from beyond the sea on this side Syria; and, behold, they be in Hazazontamar, which is Engedi. And Jehoshaphat feared, and set himself to seek the LORD, and proclaimed a fast throughout all Judah. And Judah gathered themselves together, to ask help of the LORD: even out of all the cities of Judah they came to seek the LORD. ~ II Chronicles 20:1-4

We have looked at believers and heavenly beings creating—in their worship and praise—*Glory Atmosphere* in various settings from the Old Testament to the New Testament. From Isaiah's experience in the temple, the dedication of the temple, the upper room, to Paul and Silas's inner prison revival. But what about the *great battles* of life? The times of *spiritual warfare* when the enemy has come upon us like a flood? The times when all odds are against us and overwhelmingly so? Are we to worship God for the mere sake of personal encouragement, and a boost to our *spiritual psyche*? Or does it really change the atmosphere and environment of our situation? I am convinced by the authority of the scriptures it does!

Perhaps no greater example can be found than in the Old Testament account when the pagan enemies of God had surrounded Judah. When King Jehoshaphat received news that the armies of Moab, Ammon, and Mount Sier were surrounding all of Judah the Bible states, "he feared." That is the natural reaction of any heart receiving such news. He became afraid because he knew Judah was badly outnumbered, and he could not look to other nations for help. So he does the wisest thing a believer could do. He enters into the House of God to seek the Lord. Not him only, but he sends for all of Judah to come, and join him—every man, woman, and child.

> **And Jehoshaphat feared, and set himself to seek the LORD, and proclaimed a fast throughout all Judah. And Judah gathered themselves together, to ask help of the LORD: even out of all the cities of Judah they came to seek the LORD. And Jehoshaphat stood in the congregation of Judah and Jerusalem, in the house of the LORD, before the new court. ~ II Chronicles 20:3-5**

All of Judah gathered to fast, pray, seek, and worship the Lord! I have no doubt if God's people would use that formula today, every battle we face would be won!

Jehoshaphat knew that if there was going to be a good ending to this, God was going to have to show up. Somehow this wise king knew for God to show up, the atmosphere had to be different and conducive for the presence of God. Was he led of the Spirit? It is for certain the Holy Spirit was in their midst as they gathered there, as the scriptures will confirm.

Some might ask, "What was wrong with the atmosphere in the beginning of their convocation?" There is no doubt it was one of fear for the Bible states this wise king "feared." Fear is a hindrance to faith. It is most difficult to trust and believe God when fear is present. I am certain that the *fear factor* was present in the hearts of all of Judah, for they had heard the stories of what the Ammonites, Moabites, and children of Mount Sier did to the people of the nations they invaded. Once the armies of Judah had been overwhelmed and destroyed, the pagans would come into the cities to torture and murder the young men and boys. They would rape the women and young girls, and do unspeakable things to them. It was certain in their minds that they were so outnumbered, they were about to face torture and slaughter in the coming days unless God showed up. This is no doubt the kind of atmosphere permeating the House of God as they first gathered together.

So, how is the atmosphere to change? Jehoshaphat begins to pray a prayer, not just of petition, but also of praise and acknowledgement of the greatness of God.

O LORD God of our fathers, art not Thou God in heaven? and rulest not Thou over all the kingdoms of the heathen? and in Thine hand is there not power and might, so that none is able to withstand Thee? Art not Thou our God, who didst drive out the inhabitants of this land before Thy people Israel, and gavest it to the seed of Abraham Thy friend forever? And they dwelt therein, and have built Thee a sanctuary therein for Thy name, saying, If, when evil cometh upon us, as the sword, judgment, or pestilence, or famine, we stand before this house, and in Thy presence, (for Thy name

is in this house,) and cry unto Thee in our affliction, then Thou wilt hear and help. And now, behold, the children of Ammon and Moab and mount Seir, whom Thou wouldest not let Israel invade, when they came out of the land of Egypt, but they turned from them, and destroyed them not; Behold, I say, how they reward us, to come to cast us out of Thy possession, which Thou hast given us to inherit. O our God, wilt Thou not judge them? for we have no might against this great company that cometh against us; neither know we what to do: but our eyes are upon Thee.
~ II Chronicles 20:6-12

It seems that he is asking God for confirmation concerning His mighty acts of the past, His present ability, and His promises to those who humbly come into the temple to seek Him and call on His mighty name! Yet these weren't questions to garner a *yes* from God that all this is true. But it was acknowledgment, and a declaration that they know and trust Jehovah, and are fully aware of what He's done in the past and will continue to do.

When we acknowledge and declare the attributes, the abilities, trustworthiness, and greatness of God in our prayers, we are giving Him Glory. As we do, an atmosphere is created where the presence of God can dwell and manifest Himself. Did their prayer and praise change the atmosphere here in the House of God? Absolutely! As they stood there with adoring, trusting, and praising hearts something happened, the Holy Spirit showed up.

Then upon Jahaziel the son of Zechariah, the son of Benaiah, the son of Jeiel, the son of Mattaniah, a Levite of the sons of Asaph, came the Spirit of the LORD in the midst of the congregation; And he said, Hearken ye, all Judah, and ye inhabitants of Jerusalem, and thou king Jehoshaphat, Thus saith the LORD unto you, Be not

afraid nor dismayed by reason of this great multitude; for the battle is not yours, but God's. To morrow go ye down against them: behold, they come up by the cliff of Ziz; and ye shall find them at the end of the brook, before the wilderness of Jeruel. Ye shall not need to fight in this battle: set yourselves, stand ye still, and see the salvation of the LORD with you, O Judah and Jerusalem: fear not, nor be dismayed; to morrow go out against them: for the LORD will be with you. ~ II Chronicles 20:14-17

Hallelujah, from bad news to good news! They just keep giving Him glory, creating a *Glory Atmosphere*, and keeping the presence of God in their midst.

And Jehoshaphat bowed his head with his face to the ground: and all Judah and the inhabitants of Jerusalem fell

before the LORD, worshipping the LORD. And the Levites, of the children of the Kohathites, and of the children of the Korhites, stood up to praise the LORD God of Israel with a loud voice on high. ~ II Chronicles 20:18-19

By giving Him glory, and creating a *Glory Atmosphere*, God inhabits their praises. He is dwelling among them. He has become their encourager. "Be not afraid nor dismayed." He has become their "captain of the host of the LORD" giving them battle plans for a battle they won't even have to fight in!

In the midst of *Glory Atmosphere* in the temple, the presence of God came to bring encouragement and instructions for the battle. Even though they weren't to be involved in the *hand-to-hand* combat, they were to be on the battlefield, dressed in their armor, and fitted with their weapons. Jehoshaphat understood. They must continue giving Him glory and creating *Glory Atmosphere* because they were about to face their enemy face-to-face. They were outnumbered greatly! God had told them He would fight their battle, and by this time, surely Jehoshaphat and Judah understood that God dwells in *Glory Atmosphere.* They would create that by giving Him glory on the battlefield!

> **And when he had consulted with the people, he appointed singers unto the LORD, and that should praise the beauty of holiness, as they went out before the army, and to say, Praise the LORD; for his mercy endureth for ever.**
> **~ II Chronicles 20:21**

If one could only have been close enough to witness the confusion and hear the excited conversation between the captains of the Moabites, Ammonites, and Mount Seir; "What on earth are these Jews doing? We see their archers, their swordsmen, and those who throw the spears, all in position, all in their ranks, but who is that out front? What are those weapons that they are holding? What is that strange colorful armor they are wearing? What are those scrolls they are holding up, where they seem to be reading something off them?" I can imagine one of the captains saying, "Is this some strange new type of warfare, or are they playing with our minds?" There had to be confusion, bewilderment, and questions!

Then one of the younger men with better eyesight speaks up, "Sir, those strange weapons, those scrolls they are holding up, look like Jewish songbooks! Sir, that colorful armor you see is identical to the robes the choirs of Judah wear when they sing praises to their God Jehovah in the temple on their Sabbath day!" "What," I can hear the pagan captain cry, "are you telling me that in front of their archers, swordsmen, and spear throwers are the temple singers and the temple choir?" "Yes Captain, our military intelligence tells us, 'out in front of the army is the choir!'"

About that time, "...when they began to sing and to praise," Judah's band began to play, and the singers began to sing! What were they singing? It was NOT *I'm on the battlefield for my Lord*, but *Praise the LORD, for His mercy endureth for ever, praise the beauty of holiness*. They began to give Him glory, and *Glory Atmosphere* filled the valley.

And when they began to sing and to praise, the LORD set ambushments against the children of Ammon, Moab, and mount Seir, which were come against Judah; and they were smitten. ~ II Chronicles 20:22

Jehovah pulled his chariot up, and Judah never had to draw a sword or throw a spear. Their enemies turned and slew each other in confusion!

We as the people of God must return to *biblical* worship where we worship Him in spirit and in truth with hearts filled with love and adoration for our God. If, when we are assembled together, or even when we are alone begin to give Him glory and honor, and create an atmosphere that He will inhabit, things will begin to happen in our lives, ministries, and churches for the glory of God! It will impact our prayer life, our witnessing, our daily lives, and our church services. I'm convinced that the presence of a Holy God will come to save, heal, and deliver! As we lift Him up and give Him glory, people will be drawn to His presence and revival will be a way of life. Till the day we see Him face-to-face, and live in Glory Atmosphere forever!

CONCLUSION
Chapter X

In the summer of 1980, I was conducting my first *church revival* in the church where I was raised up as a child, and where—in November of 1978—I was born again and delivered from drug addiction at nineteen years of age. It was July and I had only been officially preaching since March. Though I lacked greatly in theological training, I knew beyond a shadow of a doubt I had been called and anointed to preach the word of God.

On the first night of the meeting—which was Sunday—the attendance was above normal. Many visitors from the surrounding churches had come to hear this former drug pusher/addict preach. I had prepared a sermon on praising and worshiping God, and had taken my text from Psalm 85:6, "Wilt Thou not revive us again: that Thy people may rejoice in Thee?" I had memorized a few scriptures on praise and worship, and had written down some others to refer to during the message. Needless to say, this twenty-one year old *country boy* preacher wasn't very impressive. I read my text and began to expound in an elementary way David's plea to Jehovah to revive His people so they would again have liberty to rejoice and worship the God of Israel. I would quote a verse or read it from my simple notes, and then make some comments concerning praise and worship.

After these many years, I cannot remember just how far into the message I had gotten before something out of the ordinary for the church where I was preaching began to take place. I must say that it wasn't unusual for the people here to worship God during the services, but what happened this particular night was different.

After several minutes into the preaching, all of a sudden a group in one part of the church just stood up in unison, raised their hands, and began to worship God. Then after a few moments they would be seated again. I would read another verse about praise and begin to preach again. After some minutes would pass, another group would suddenly jump to their feet, raise their hands, and begin to praise and worship God with all their hearts. Then again after a few moments, they would sit back down and I would continue. After about the third or fourth time of this spontaneous outburst of jubilant praise and worship, it was obvious that something supernatural and wonderful was taking place.

If I had known then about how God's people create *Glory Atmosphere* with their worship and praise, then what happened next wouldn't have been such a surprise. No doubt when those groups began to jump up and worship the Creator of heaven and earth with all their hearts, their worship began to ascend up like an incense to the Throne Room of heaven, to the very nostrils of God! I don't know if it was before what happened next or during, but I'm convinced Adonai called for His chariot! I can almost hear the Angel say, "Where are you going Most High and Holy God of heaven and earth?" And if my earthly ears could have heard the reply, "The sweet aroma of praise is coming up from a group of my children, and I'm going down to dwell in it!"

Hallelujah! That group of believers along with myself didn't see the chariot when it pulled up, but I can look back now and remember when it arrived.

After these three or four episodes of spontaneous worship, all of a sudden, without anyone asking or suggesting, in unison, the whole congregation stood to their feet. With hands raised toward heaven, they began to praise and worship God in a way I don't think I've seen before, or since anywhere. The sound of praise would rise and fall like the *voice of many waters* and the *voice of mighty thunderings!* It was like *waves* of the Holy Spirit would move across the congregation.

I honestly cannot say for certain how long this lasted, but it seemed over half an hour or more. Though we did not fully understand it then, we were giving Him Glory and therefore creating a *Glory Atmosphere* for God Almighty to come and inhabit. This could not have been planned nor orchestrated. This was the Holy Ghost revealing to His people the supernatural reality of what happens when the saints worship Him in Spirit and in truth without the conscious limitations of a time clock, or some gifted orator consciously or unconsciously motivating the worshippers. It was redeemed men, women, and young people with tears running down their faces, thankful hearts, and hands raised giving glory and worshipping the Redeemer of their souls! It was the Lamb that was slain from before the foundations of the world coming to dwell in the *Glory Atmosphere* created in these humble hearts gathered inside a small church building in Tennessee. Only heaven knows how many were saved from sin, healed physically and spiritually, delivered, and baptized in the Holy Ghost that Sunday night when God showed up to dwell in *Glory Atmosphere!*

With all the emphasis on praise and worship today, why doesn't this happen more often?

It's the *heart*. Motive is everything. When we cease to worship *the worship* and *worship leaders,* begin to truly worship God in spirit and in truth, when with pure hearts and clean hands we come together and begin to give Him glory due unto His name creating a *Glory Atmosphere*, then listen for the rumbling of the chariot wheels!

He is coming to dwell in the praises of His people!

CPSIA information can be obtained at www.ICGtesting.com
Printed in the USA
LVOW01s2144240715

447538LV00001B/2/P